TIMBA
THE TIGER

TRUE-TO-LIFE BOOKS
Educating children about endangered species

Photographed by Jan Davis and Jon Resnick
Written by Jon Resnick
Designed and produced by Jan Davis

Hi, my name is Timba. I am a Bengal tiger.
I live in India in a beautiful forest.

Meet Tickles, my sister. We were born in a cave.
We weighed only one kilo each. My mother will care
for us until we are around two years old.
Then we will go off on our own.

Each tiger has its own home range. My daddy covers an area of around 100 sq. km. My mummy has a much smaller range of around 40 sq.km.

We spend most of the day sleeping or resting.
Towards sunset we become active.
At night we do most of our hunting.

Tigers are built to hunt.
We have powerful jaws, knife-like claws...

sharp teeth... keen eyesight...

a good sense of smell... and excellent hearing to help us pinpoint prey.

How do we catch our prey?

Usually we sneak up on them. We crouch down on our bellies and crawl very slowly. Sometimes it takes 30 minutes to cover a short distance.

Then we charge and pounce.
About one hunt in twenty is successful.

Tigers are carnivores, which means we eat meat.
We can eat up to 35 kilos of meat at one time.
That is more than 300 hamburgers!

No wonder tigers are the largest of the cat family.
A full-grown daddy can reach 300 kilos, but
a mummy is smaller, around 150 kilos.

Do you like my stripes? I use them for camouflage. No two tigers have the same pattern of stripes. In fact, my stripes are not even the same on both sides of my body.

Look closely. Can you tell us apart? The markings on our foreheads are all different.

Tigers have different ways of communicating with each other.

We leave our scent behind by spraying trees…

rubbing trees...

and hugging trees.

We also leave claw marks on trees.

When we smell another tiger, we make a face by wrinkling our nose and opening our mouth. We can tell who was there before us with just one sniff.

We also communicate by making different sounds. We pant, growl, cry, hiss, scream, snarl, purr and, of course, roar.

We are very good swimmers, but we don't like to get our face wet. We usually enter the water rear first.

Tigers walk on the soft pads of their toes. There are five on the front feet and four on the back feet.

Our footprints are called pug marks. Can you see the pug mark I left behind?

Tigers like to play and groom, just like house cats.

Tigers first arrived on Earth about one to two million years ago. There were eight different kinds. Sadly, three of them have become extinct in the last 50 years. The others are now in great danger from humans.

Today, there are only around 5,000 tigers left in the wild. People are killing us for our skin, fat and bones. In Asia, every part of the tiger is used in traditional medicines. People are also killing our prey and destroying our habitat.

TIGER FACTS

SCIENTIFIC NAME: Panthera tigris

TIGER SUBSPECIES: Bengal, Indochinese, Sumatran, Siberian, South China, Bali, Caspian and Javan, but the last three are now extinct. The others are in great danger of vanishing from the earth.

HABITAT: Tigers are very adaptable and live in many different kinds of habitats in Asia: snow-capped mountains, steamy jungles, grassy meadows, swamps, bamboo groves, and river valleys.

WEIGHT: Male up to 300 kilos, female up to 160 kilos.

LENGTH: Male up to 4 metres from nose to tip of tail and female up to 2.7 metres.

HEIGHT: About 1 metre to the shoulder.

CLAWS & CANINES: Claws as long as 10cm. The two upper canine teeth as long as 7.6cm.

DIET: Tigers kill to eat. They hunt everything from grasshoppers to elephants, including deer, monkeys, wild pigs, porcupines, crocodiles, snakes and crabs.

PREDATORS: Mainly humans. Sometimes wild dogs, elephants, bears, jackals and hyenas attack the young. Also, one tiger will kill another over territory or a mate.

LIFE SPAN: Up to 20 years in the wild and 25 in captivity.

NUMBERS REMAINING (estimate)

Bengal - 3,250

Indochinese - 1,200

Sumatran - 450

Siberian - 150

South China - 25

Bali - extinct since 1940s

Caspian - extinct since 1970s

Javan - extinct since 1980s

DID YOU KNOW?

- A tiger's stripes are permanent, like a birthmark.
- Tigers have the pulling power of 30 men.
- Tigers are colour-blind.
- Tigers and lions have mated, creating tigons or ligers.

SUGGESTED READING

BENGAL TIGER (Animals in Danger)
Rod Theodorou, 2000

BIG CATS (Nature Fact Files)
Rhonda Klevansky, 2000

HOW THE TIGER LOST ITS STRIPES:
AN EXPLANATION INTO THE ENDANGERMENT
OF A SPECIES Cory J. Meacham, 1997

RIDING THE TIGER: TIGER CONSERVATION
IN HUMAN-DOMINATED LANDSCAPES
John Seidensticker, 1999

SECRET LIFE OF TIGERS Valmik Thapar, 1999

THE TIGER (Endangered Animals & Habitats)
Stuart P. Levine, 1998

TIGER (Natural World Series)
Bill Jordan, Valmik Thapar, 1999

TIGER: HABITATS, LIFE CYCLES, FOOD CHAINS,
THREATS Valmik Thapar, 1999

TIGERS Susan Schafer, 2000

TIGERS IN THE SNOW Peter Matthiessen, 2000

TRACK OF THE TIGER:
LEGEND & LORE OF THE GREAT CAT
Maurice Hornocker, 1997

THE YEAR OF THE TIGER
Geoffrey C. Ward, Michael Nichols, 1998

INTERESTING WEBSITES

ALL FOR TIGERS www.tiger.to

CARNIVORE PRESERVATION TRUST
www.cptigers.org

CAT SPECIALIST GROUP
www.lynx.uio.no./catfolk

INTERNET TIGER ACTIVISTS
www.savetigers.com

KID'S PLANET www.kidsplanet.org

PLIGHT OF THE INDIAN TIGER www.nbs.it/tiger

SAVE THE TIGER FUND www.nfwf.org/stf.htm

THE TIGER FOUNDATION www.tigerfdn.com

THE TIGER INFORMATION CENTER
www.5tigers.org

THE WORLD CONSERVATION UNION
www.iucn.org

TIGER MISSING LINK FOUNDATION
www.tigerlink.org

TIGER TERRITORY
www.loadstar.prometeus.net/tiger

TIGER TRAILS www.ips.net/tenil/tiger.htm

WORLD WIDE FUND FOR NATURE www.wwf.org